THE NEW

REVISED A

ETHNICITY AND IMMIGRATION

JAMES P. SHENTON
AND KEVIN KENNY

AMERICAN HISTORICAL ASSOCIATION

James P. Shenton is professor of history at Columbia University. Among his books are *Robert John Walker: A Politician from Jackson to Lincoln* and *A Historian's History of the United States*.

Kevin Kenny is assistant professor of history at the University of Texas at Austin, where his area of specialization is U.S. social history. He is the author of *Making Sense of the Molly Maguires*.

This essay originally appeared in *The New American History (Revised and Expanded Edition)*, published by Temple University Press in the series Critical Perspectives on the Past, edited by Susan Porter Benson, Stephen Brier, and Roy Rosenzweig.
Copyright © 1997 Temple University.

This edition published by the American Historical Association
Cover design by Amy Smith Bell
ISBN: 0-87229-087-5
Printed in the United States of America

Contents

Preface to the Revised and Expanded Edition	v
Introduction to the First Edition	vii
Ethnicity and Immigration	1
The First Immigrants	2
The "Old" Immigrants	4
The "New" Immigrants	6
Nativism and Immigration Restriction	9
Assimilation and Anglo-Conformity	10
A World in Migration: The Newest Immigrants	14
Bibliography	15

Preface to the Revised and Expanded Edition

IN THE YEARS SINCE *THE NEW AMERICAN HISTORY* WAS PUBLISHED IN 1990, THE study and teaching of history unexpectedly emerged as the subject of intense public debate. For a time, one could scarcely open a newspaper without encountering bitter controversy over the public presentation of the American past. Previously uncontroversial historical anniversaries became occasions for heated debate. The ambiguity that marked the quincentenary of Columbus's voyage to the New World, for example, contrasted dramatically with the unembarrassed celebration of its four hundredth anniversary a century earlier. No one in the 1890s seemed to doubt that 1492 marked an epochal moment in the progress of human civilization, while in 1992, the celebration was tempered by constant reminders of chattel slavery, the decimation of native populations, and other less than glorious consequences. Three years later, a proposed exhibition at the National Air and Space Museum to mark the fiftieth anniversary of the dropping of the first atomic bomb produced howls of outrage from veterans organizations, who charged that initial plans cast the Japanese of the Second World War as innocent victims rather than aggressors. The pressure exerted by these organizations, augmented by the threat of a reduction in congressional funding, forced the curators to rewrite the exhibition script to highlight Japan's wartime atrocities and remove documents revealing that high military officials in 1945 had doubted the need for using the bomb.

Simultaneously, controversy erupted over proposed national standards for history education drawn up with the participation of hundreds of scholars and every major professional association of history teachers. Critics condemned the plan for neglecting great figures of the American past like George Washington, and, more broadly, for adopting an excessively uncelebratory tone in dealing with the nation's history.

Whatever the outcome of these debates—and one hopes that when the smoke has cleared, it will leave behind a heightened public interest in an understanding of history—the transformation of historical scholarship that inspired the original publication of *The New American History* has proceeded apace. This revised edition includes essays on three fields that have undergone extremely dramatic changes of late. The new essays—on intellectual history, Western history, and the history of the family and of sexuality—examine current thinking in three of the most creative subfields in American historical writing. As for the original essays, nearly all have been revised (and some entirely rewritten) to bring the texts and bibliographies up to date. Taken together, the new and revised essays reflect the continuing vitality and creativity of the study of the American past, how traditional fields are being expanded and redefined even as new ones are created.

ERIC FONER
Columbia University

■■ Introduction to the First Edition

IN THE COURSE OF THE PAST TWENTY YEARS, AMERICAN HISTORY HAS BEEN remade. Inspired initially by the social movements of the 1960s and 1970s—which shattered the "consensus" vision that had dominated historical writing—and influenced by new methods borrowed from other disciplines, American historians redefined the very nature of historical study. The rise of the "new histories," the emphasis on the experience of ordinary Americans, the impact of quantification and cultural analysis, the eclipse of conventional political and intellectual history—these trends are now so widely known (and the subject of such controversy) that they need little reiteration. The study of American history today looks far different than it did a generation ago.

This series comprises essays written by thirteen scholars—many of whom have been at the forefront of the transformation of historical study—each assessing recent developments in historians' understanding of a period or a major theme in the nation's past. The idea for the collection originated with a request from the American Historical Association for a series of pamphlets addressed specifically to high school teachers of American history and designed to familiarize them with the most up-to-date historical scholarship. High school teachers, the association believed, sense that the study of history has changed dramatically of late; overwhelmed as they are with classroom responsibilities, however, they have little time for extensive reading and are unable to keep up with all the trends in research and interpretation.

After a false start or two the proposal, somewhat revised, was adopted and published as a collection by Temple University Press, and now, separately, by the AHA. *The New American History* is addressed to a wide audience: students, teachers, and the broad public concerned with the current state of American historical study.

Each author was given a free hand in developing his or her reflections. No attempt has been made to fit the essays into a predetermined mold or impose a single point of view or interpretive framework. Nonetheless, certain themes recur with remarkable regularity, demonstrating how pervasively the "new histories" have reshaped our understanding of the American past.

If anything is characteristic of the recent study of American history, it is attention to the experience of previously neglected groups—not simply as an addition to a preexisting body of knowledge but as a fundamental redefinition of history itself. Women's history has greatly expanded its subject area, moving beyond the movement for suffrage, which preoccupied earlier women historians, into such previously ignored realms as the history of sexuality. Labor history, from a field that defined its subject as the experience of wage workers in factories and the activities of unionized workers, has expanded to encompass the study of slaves, women at home, and the majority of laborers, who in America have always been unorganized.

Even more striking, perhaps, is that African-American history and women's history have matured to the point where they are not widely recognized as legitimate subfields with their own paradigms and debates but are seen as indispensable to any understanding of the broad American experience. These points are made effectively in surveys of the two fields by Thomas Holt and Linda Gordon, but they are evident in other contributions as well. Richard McCormick makes clear that any calculus of Americans' gains and losses in the late nineteenth and early twentieth centuries must take into account the severe reverses suffered by blacks in those years. William Chafe places the civil rights movement at the center of his analysis of social change in post–World War II America. My own essay on the Civil War era argues not only that slavery and emancipation were the central issues in the sectional crisis but that blacks were active agents in shaping the era's history.

Women's history, too, has forced historians not simply to compensate for their previous neglect of one-half of the population but to rethink some of their basic premises. John Murrin explains why the study of family structure is essential to an understanding of colonial society. Linda Kerber delineates how the American Revolution affected prevailing definitions of "manhood" and "womanhood" and how patriarchy itself was restructured as a result of the revolutionary crisis. Leon Fink emphasizes the obvious but long-ignored fact that women have always been part of the country's labor history. Sean Wilentz shows that a key result of economic changes in the Jacksonian era was an ideological division between the public sphere of men and the private sphere of women.

Many of the essays also demonstrate the impact of new methods on recent historical study. John Murrin shows how historical demography has yielded a new estimate of the human toll exacted by the colonization of the New World and how epidemiology affects our understanding of the decimation of the hemisphere's original inhabitants. Alice Kessler-Harris outlines the ways in which the "new empiricism" of statistical analysis has helped shape developments in social history. Richard McCormick and Alan Brinkley assess the impact of modernization theory on the study of both pre- and post-World War I periods.

Despite the apparent ascendancy of social history, these essays do not lend credence to recent complaints that historians are no longer concerned with politics, economics, the Constitution, and intellectual history. Such traditional concerns appear in virtually every essay, although often in forms that earlier historians might find unrecognizable. The old "presidential synthesis"—which understood the evolution of American society chiefly via presidential elections and administrations—is dead (and not lamented). And "politics" now means much more than the activities of party leaders. Some essays devote attention to the broad political culture or "public life" of a particular era; others stress the role of the state itself in American history and the ways various groups have tried to use it for their own purposes.

Alan Brinkley, for example, discusses the New Deal within the context of the constraints imposed on government by the nature of America's political and economic institutions, and the general impact of the period on the evolution of the American state. And Walter LaFeber shows how the Constitution has helped to shape the evolution of American foreign policy.

Many historians have lamented of late the failure of the current generation of scholars to produce a modern "synthesis" of the American past. Older synthetic interpretations, ranging from Frederick Jackson Turner's frontier thesis to the consensus view of the 1950s, have been shattered, but no new one has emerged to fill the void. Indeed, the very diversity of the "new histories" and the portrait of America they have created seem to have fragmented historical scholarship and impeded the attempt to create a coherent new vision of the national experience. Several of the essays echo this concern, but there is sufficient similarity in their approaches and interpretations to suggest that the fragmentation of historical study may have been overstated. If the essays do not, and by their very nature cannot, produce the widely called-for new synthesis, several do point in that direction. Sean Wilentz, for example, suggests that the social, political, and economic history of Jacksonian America can be integrated into a coherent whole by placing the market revolution at the center of the account. Richard McCormick demonstrates that a "public life" can be a flexible, imaginative concept, capable of integrating a variety of social, economic, and political developments.

As this series demonstrates, American history is a field of remarkable diversity and vitality. Its practitioners continue to grapple with the most pressing issues and persistent themes of our national experience: definitions of liberty and equality, causes of social change, the exercise of political power. Today, popular knowledge—or lack of knowledge—of the nation's past has once again become a subject of intense public discussion. Certainly, the more all of us—students, teachers, and other citizens—know of our national experience, the better. But as these essays illustrate, American history at its best remains not simply a collection of facts, not a politically sanctioned listing of indisputable "truths," but an ongoing mode of collective self-discovery about the nature of our society.

ERIC FONER
Columbia University

ETHNICITY AND IMMIGRATION

*James P. Shenton
and Kevin Kenny*

IMMIGRATION IS ONCE AGAIN A SIGNIFICANT ASPECT OF AMERICAN LIFE. THE LATINO population of the United States has almost tripled since 1960, reaching 20 million in 1990. The Asian population reached 7.3 million in the same year, the majority from Korea, China and, more recently, India. In the 1980s alone, 7 million immigrants entered the United States legally, more than for any decade in American history except 1901–10, when 8.8 million arrived. And, if an estimated average of 300,000 to 500,000 undocumented aliens a year is added to the figures, the total for the 1980s exceeds that for 1901–10 and becomes the highest in American history. These new immigrants are not as high a proportion of the total population as they once were (12 percent in the 1850s, 11 percent in the 1900s, and at most 3 percent in the 1980s), but an era of mass migration to the United States has returned and with it a national debate over culture, history, language and immigration restriction.

In the light of these developments, historians have begun to reappraise the history of American immigration and ethnicity as a whole. Considerable attention has been paid to the newest immigrants from Asia and Latin America. The history of immigration in the colonial period and in the nineteenth and early twentieth centuries has also been reconsidered and revised. In place of an old picture dominated by the "breakdown" of immigrant cultures and their assimilation into a dominant Anglo culture, new models of ethnicity and assimilation are beginning to emerge, calling into question traditional two-dimensional accounts of race as white versus black, of ethnicity as native-born American versus foreign-born "ethnic," and of assimilation as citizen versus alien.

THE FIRST IMMIGRANTS

According to the first federal census, taken in 1790, there were 3,172,444 whites and 757,208 blacks in the original states plus Vermont, Kentucky, and Tennessee. It is estimated that 56 percent of this population of almost 4 million were of English and Scottish origin, 19 percent of African origin, 8 percent Irish (just over half of whom were Scotch-Irish Protestants from Ulster), 7 percent German, and the remainder from Holland, France, Sweden, and elsewhere. Estimates of the total number of people who migrated to the United States before 1819, when the federal government first required ships' captains to report the number of debarking passengers, have been educated guesses at best.

There were significant differences between the immigrants who settled the Chesapeake Bay area and those who settled New England. The Puritan migration of the 1630s generally consisted of stable, relatively prosperous family groups. The Chesapeake, by contrast, attracted larger numbers of single males, typically poorer than their northern peers, and lacking the discipline and social cohesiveness provided by Puritanism. If they were not the "whores, rogues and vagabonds" described by a previous generation of historians, significant numbers of the immigrants to the southern colonies came from the lower orders of British society. Desperate for men and women who could work, these colonies were prepared to import convict labor, as Roger Ekirch has described in his study of 50,000 convicts transported to the American colonies in the eighteenth century. But convicts were the exception; and, even in the southern colonies, immigrants were not the "dregs" of British society but a representative cross-section of its lower and middle orders. David Galenson, for example, has demonstrated that the indentured servants who made up the bulk of the immigrant population in the colonial period were skilled artisans, healthy teenage boys, practicing farmers, and landless laborers in need of work.

Immigrants may have been "pushed" out of their homelands for economic, political, religious, military, and even biological reasons, but there was an equally strong set of "pull" factors enticing them to come to the United States. Many of these pull factors were simply the mirror images of the forces pushing the immigrants out of their homelands: the possibility of becoming rich or at least economically comfortable, the availability of land, religious and political freedom. Some of these expectations proved exaggerated, others illusory. A genuinely transatlantic approach to the history of American immigration in the colonial era must start with a thorough understanding of the push factors at home; move from there to the pull factors and the extent to which they were real; and, on that basis, examine patterns of settlement, culture, and assimilation. One step in that direction is the recent work of Bernard Bailyn on the lives and aspirations of tens of thousands of anonymous emigrants who left Britain for America in the 1770s. Most of them did so, he concludes, less for reasons of war, plague, poverty, or persecution than out of attraction to "this strange world" across the Atlantic Ocean.

The British and Irish domination of immigration from Europe in the colonial period should not blind us to the considerable diversity and contentiousness among the newcomers. While more indentured servants settled in the southern than the northern colonies, the fundamental fact about the former region is that servants coexisted with large numbers of slaves, brought to the United States involuntarily from the Caribbean and Africa. And, if Puritan New England was the most homogenous American region until the arrival of the Irish in the 1830s, it retained its purity only at the price of banishing heretics and hanging proselytizing Quakers. As for other ethnic groups, there were about 100,000 Americans of Dutch birth or descent in the United States in 1790, 80,000 of them within a fifty-mile radius of New York City. Between 75,000 and 100,000 German immigrants are estimated to have arrived during the colonial period, concentrating in Pennsylvania but settling along the East Coast as far south as Georgia. And, though the number of French immigrants in the colonial period is unknown, it included 14,000 Huguenot refugees who came to the future United States and another 10,000 Roman Catholics who settled in Canada. During the French Revolution, 10,000 more refugees came to the United States, many from the Caribbean islands.

The Middle Colonies were the most ethnically diverse and religiously tolerant. If this was true of William Penn's Philadelphia, it was all the more true of New York City, as Randall Balmer has explained. Tensions between the Dutch and the English residents of the city peaked in 1664 and again in 1689–91, when Dutch artisans and small shopkeepers fought unsuccessfully against English rulers and their allies in the Dutch merchant class. Thereafter, New York was to be an English colony, but it lost none of its diversity. According to one report, eighteen languages were being spoken there as early as 1643.

Despite its diversity and its centrality in subsequent national development, excessive attention to the Northeast obscures the nature of migration and ethnicity in colonial North America as a whole. While the position of Native Americans and African Americans in the colonial period is considered elsewhere in this volume, greater attention is needed to Spanish colonization and, above all, to people of Spanish and Mexican Indian origin in the Southwest. The standard work is still John Bannon's history of the Spanish borderlands from the sixteenth through the early nineteenth centuries. Among the most readable accounts of the deep-rooted Mexican presence in the Southwest is John Chavez's account of the Chicano image of a "Lost Land." But the outstanding work on this early period is Ramón Gutiérrez's powerful and evocative account of the Pueblo Indians of New Mexico from the arrival of the Spanish in the sixteenth century to the Anglo conquest three centuries later, viewed through the lens of power, religion, sexuality, and marriage. With themes as rich as these, the history of the borderlands is fast becoming one of the most exciting subfields in American ethnic history.

THE "OLD" IMMIGRANTS

Historians typically use the term "old" immigration for the period 1820 and 1880, and "new" immigration for the period 1880 to the 1920s. This terminology has recently become outdated, as the genuinely "new" immigration is the one that has occurred in the United States since 1965. Nonetheless, it retains some usefulness for historiography by differentiating the two great waves of immigration to the United States in the century after 1820.

The "old" immigration brought more than 10 million immigrants to the United States in a sixty-year period, with the greatest activity between 1840 and 1860, when almost 4.5 million arrived. The first to arrive in large numbers were the Irish, almost 5 million of whom traveled to the United States between 1820 and 1920, a figure exceeded only by the Germans. Their passage to America has been memorably portrayed by Kerby Miller, whose work throws down a gauntlet to historians of American immigration and ethnicity in general by insisting that the immigrants' world in America makes little sense unless we begin with a thorough understanding of the world they left behind. This Miller does to great effect for the Irish, though not without formulating a thesis guaranteed to ruffle the feathers of many Irish Americans. The Irish, Miller argues, were deeply damaged by the forces of "modernization" (colonial conquest, capitalist agriculture, the beginnings of industry and urbanization) and arrived in the United States ill-equipped to cope with the harsh and often bewildering nature of industrial life. Falling back on a rich, preliterate Gaelic culture, they tended to interpret their emigration not as voluntary self-improvement but as exile and banishment. It was a short step from there to blaming the British for the whole thing, and it was no accident that the United States became in the late nineteenth century the most fertile source of ideas, munitions, men, and money for the struggle to win independence in Ireland.

The other group that accounted for significant numbers of the "old" immigrants were the Germans. They typically arrived in family units, in contrast to the young single men and women who came from Ireland. And they arrived through New Orleans as well as the eastern cities, generally moving on into the interior. About 1 million Germans came to the United States in the 1840s and 1850s; more than 3 million between 1860 and 1900; and another 1.3 million by 1924. Catholics dominated the first wave, but Protestants, especially from Prussia, were increasingly numerous thereafter. The Germans tended to arrive with some money and skills, unlike the Irish, many of whom had neither, especially in the 1840s and 1850s. Thus, while the typical German immigrant became a farmer, artisan, or shopkeeper, the typical male Irish immigrant (Paddy) became an unskilled laborer and the typical female Irish immigrant (Bridget) became a domestic servant or, later, a factory worker. German immigration lacks a synthesis in the grand style produced by Kerby Miller for the Irish. But fine regional studies have been written by Walter Kamphoefner on Westfalians in Missouri and by Stanley Nadel on German ethnicity, religion, and class in New York City's kleindeutschland. Bruce Levine's work examines the impact of German immigrants, infused with the revolutionary spirit of 1848, on the antebellum labor movement and the antislavery crusade.

The great anomaly among the old "immigrants" were the Chinese, 322,000 of whom arrived in the United States between 1850 and 1882. Nearly all of them were males between the ages of 14 and 35; they worked primarily on railroad construction on contracts drawn up before they arrived; and they settled on the West rather than the East Coast. The typical Chinese railroad laborer contracted to work for six to eight years, with the hope of accumulating cash and returning to China. The Contract Labor Law of 1865 had allowed for such contracts, but they were outlawed by the Contract Labor Law of 1885. The importance of the Chinese to the history of American migration lies partly in the labor they performed on railroad construction and partly in the precedent they set as the first immigrant group to be excluded from entry to the United States. The impetus to restrict the Chinese came in part from a widespread and deeply racist belief that they could never assimilate into American life. Related to this, as Alexander Saxton has explained, was a fear on the part of organized labor, led ironically enough by recent immigrants from Ireland, that cheap Chinese labor was a major threat to the welfare of "American" workers. The Chinese Exclusion Act of 1882 suspended the entry of Chinese laborers for ten years; it was re-enacted in 1892 and 1902, and in 1904 the ban was extended indefinitely.

The nineteenth century also witnessed ongoing struggles between the Mexican residents of the Southwest and migrating Anglo-Americans, culminating in the annexation of half of Mexico's national territory (including Texas) in the 1840s. Arnoldo de Léon has written an impressive account of the racial discrimination faced by Texans of Mexican origin (*tejanos*); while David Montejano places the categories of race and class at the center of Texan history since 1836, in an ambitious and influential work of revisionist history. Useful community studies for the nineteenth and twentieth centuries include Albert Camarillo's work on Santa Barbara and southern California from 1848 to 1930; Gilberto Hinojosa's account of the transformation of the border town of Laredo from 1755 to 1870; Mario Garcia's work on the Mexicans of El Paso between 1880 and 1920; and studies of East Los Angeles by Rodolfo Acuña and Ricardo Romo. Perhaps the most theoretically innovative work has been on issues of gender and the family. Rebecca Craver's work, for example, deals with Mexican-Anglo intermarriage in New Mexico in the early nineteenth century. Richard Griswold del Castillo examines the tensions accompanying migration and assimilation in the Chicano family since 1848. And Sarah Deutsch analyzes the cultural interaction, particularly in terms of gender, between Latinos, Anglos, and Native Americans in New Mexico and Colorado from 1880 to 1940.

THE "NEW" IMMIGRANTS

Between 1880 and 1924, almost 27,000,000 white immigrants entered the United States. Locating this great migration in the context of global movements of labor and capital, John Bodnar has provided something of a blueprint for studying this "new" immigration as a whole. Two-thirds of the "new" immigrants came from parts of central, eastern, and southern Europe that were economically underdeveloped and politically regressive. Most were drawn to the booming industrial sector of the American economy, where they performed unskilled labor; but many brought skills that were vital to industries as diverse as construction and garment production. With the exception of John Bodnar's work and that of a handful of others (notably Caroline Golab, Victor Greene, Paul Krause, and Ewa Moraskawa), the literature on Slavic immigrants is surprisingly sparse.

Of all the "new" immigrants, Jews have received the most comprehensive treatment by historians. Moses Rischin's account of the social and intellectual life of New York's eastern European Jews has become a classic, thirty-five years after it was published. Irving Howe offers a massive and exuberant treatment of radicalism in the same community, while Sydney Weinberg in his recent work explores "how Jewish women sought and found meaning for their lives within the framework of their own system and values." Stephan Brumberg has demonstrated how public schools acted as an agent of "Americanization" for newcomers from central and eastern Europe. Deborah Dash Moore deals sympathetically with the stresses endured by the generation obliged to straddle two worlds, arguing that divisions between parents and children have been overstated. By contrast, John Bukowczyk's study of another "new" immigrant group, the Poles, concludes that intergenerational stresses were considerable. Elizabeth Ewen's work finds striking similarities in the lives of Jewish and Italian women on the Lower East Side. Both groups belonged to a patriarchal immigrant culture that nonetheless accorded them an autonomous women's sphere; both were rapidly "Americanized" through initiation into a consumer society that undermined traditional gender roles and opened up new, and sometimes double-edged, ways of life, work, and womanhood.

The literature on the Italians is almost as ample as that on the Jews. About 4 million immigrants came from Italy to the United States between 1899 and 1924 alone. Most arrived with a firmly rooted regional or provincial identity and came predominantly from the south. These considerations have shaped much of the recent scholarship, especially the argument that assimilation into the American environment involved a simultaneous recognition, for the first time, of a common Italian heritage. Silvano Tomasi offers a judicious account of the strains between Italian immigrants and the Irish Americans who dominated the Roman Catholic Church in New York; while Robert Orsi offers a colorful portrait of the religion practiced and performed on the streets of Italian Harlem. Betty Boyd Caroli's work examines repatriation, remarkably common among the Italians; many arrived in the United States as "birds of passage" and about 1.5 million returned to Italy in the first fifteen years of the twentieth century. Virginia Yans-McLaughlin's work on the Italians of Buffalo between 1880 and 1930 offers a detailed and sympathetic portrait of work, family life, and community in a single city, concluding that despite initial discrimination the transition from Italy to America was "relatively smooth." Finally, Donna Gabaccia's work on Sicilian labor and immigration demonstrates with great effectiveness Kerby Miller's point that the immigrants' experience cannot properly be understood without a detailed examination of the world they left behind.

Gabaccia's work raises one of the central questions in the study of immigration, its intersection with the history of labor. For most of American history it is impossible to write the history of one without writing the history of the other. This point was influentially made in the 1970s by Herbert Gutman, who demonstrated how the American working class, in contrast to the putative English model, did not undergo a single "making" but was instead repeatedly transformed by infusions of pre-industrial immigrants. The importance of a detailed knowledge of European social and political history in any account of American immigration and labor has been emphasized in a series of works by the German historian Dirk Hoerder. In a similar vein are Bruce Levine's work on mid-nineteenth-century German immigrants and Susan Glenn's study of work, family, womanhood, and trade unionism among Jewish immigrants.

The relation between ethnicity and class has been the subject of fruitful inquiry, especially in the historiography of the late nineteenth and early twentieth centuries. David Emmons emphasizes the ethnic exclusiveness and working-class "pragmatism" of Irish immigrant workers in Butte, Montana. Similarly, John Bodnar argues that east European immigrants tended to eschew radicalism by putting concerns of family, ethnic kin, and religion before larger social interests. David Montgomery concedes that the exclusion from the organized labor movement of unskilled immigrants from central, southern, and eastern Europe gravely damaged the cause of labor as whole. On the other hand, Bruce Levine, Eric Foner, David Goldberg, and others all demonstrate, in different ways, how ethnic consciousness could serve as a catalyst rather than an obstacle to class consciousness. Gary Gerstle's study of the textile town of Woonsocket, Rhode Island, explains how twentieth-century "Americanism" could be defined in working-class as well as middle-class terms, allowing French Canadians and Franco-Belgian immigrants to overcome their ethnic differences.

Some of the best recent work on the intersection of labor and immigration history examines the history of Mexican workers in the United States. Vicki Ruiz, for example, examines the struggle for unionization by Mexican women in the California cannery industry between 1930 and 1950. Zaragosa Vargas offers a penetrating analysis of Mexican industrial workers in Detroit and the Midwest between World War I and the New Deal. Emilio Zamora presents a wide-ranging account of rural and urban Mexican workers in early-twentieth-century Texas. And Camille Geurin-Gonzalez covers the world of Mexican immigration, farm labor, and repatriation in California. For Mexicans in the twentieth century, as for groups like the Irish and the Italians in the nineteenth, issues of work and class have been the essence of the immigrant experience.

Ethnicity and Immigration

NATIVISM AND IMMIGRATION RESTRICTION

One thing the "old" immigrants and the "new" faced in common was the onslaught of nativism, defined by its leading historian, John Higham, as "intense hostility to an internal minority on the grounds of its foreign (or 'un-American') connections." As the first substantial group of non-Anglo Protestants to arrive as immigrants in the United States, the Irish bore the brunt of the early attacks, a development most recently examined by Dale Knobel. The general pattern of nativism throughout American history has been analyzed by David Bennett, who argues that what "tied these movements to one tradition was the common vision of alien intruders in the promised land—people who could not be assimilated in the national community because of their religion or ethnicity."

The customs, cultures, languages, religions, and dress of the "new" immigrants struck many native-born Americans as exotic and threatening. Could they ever be assimilated into American life? This question was asked with increasing frequency beginning in the 1890s, and the attitude behind it is typified by one congressman's warning: "There may have been a time when we could assimilate this undesirable immigration—the ignorant, the pauper, and the vicious class. That time has passed. . . . They strain our public and our private charities, fill our charitable institutions, and are a constant menace to our free institutions." The varieties of nativist thought deployed against the new immigrants—anti-Catholic, antiradical, anti-Semitic, and Anglo-Saxon racist—have been delineated by John Higham in one of the classic works of American immigration history.

The movement to regulate and eventually restrict immigration grew slowly from the 1890s, eventually achieving its goals in the 1920s. The Immigration Act of 1891 excluded people with contagious diseases and mental disorders and established Ellis Island as the principal clearinghouse for the new arrivals. Certain classes of political radical were excluded under new legislation in 1903. During the next thirteen years, thirteen separate legislative acts were passed, each closing the Golden Door bit by bit. The year 1917 was a turning point, with the codification of the existing legislation and the classification of thirty-three types of aliens to be denied entrance, among them "feeble-minded" persons, persons of "constitutional psychopathic inferiority," and those who held "subversive" political views. The same year, Congress passed a literacy test for immigrants over President Woodrow Wilson's vehement veto, and a national campaign against radicalism and "un-American" sympathies reached its peak.

An unrestricted system of immigration could not have stayed in place indefinitely. But the striking thing about immigration restriction is the extent to which it was formulated in terms of racial nativism. In 1921, Congress passed an emergency immigration act, establishing a quota system by which annual immigration from any country could not exceed 3 percent of the number of persons of that nationality present in the United States in 1910. This law reduced immigration from about 800,000 to about 357,000 a year. But the nativists remained unsatisfied, demanding a 2 percent quota, based on the 1890 census, when there had been far fewer "new" immigrants in the United States. In 1924 the National Origins Act (or Johnson-Reed Immigration Act) banned immigration from East Asia entirely, reduced the quota from 3 to 2 percent (about 165,000 a year, reduced to 150,000 in 1927), and pushed the base year back from 1910 to 1890. Future immigration, in other words, was to be primarily "Nordic" or "Teutonic" in composition, and the numbers were drastically reduced. The new "national origins" system stayed in place until 1965.

ASSIMILATION AND ANGLO-CONFORMITY

The virulence of American nativism calls into question the category of "assimilation" that has typically lain at the heart of debates over immigration and ethnicity, both popular and scholarly. Early interpretations of immigrant history accepted as a given the migration of people from all over the world and considered their assimilation into American life as the central problem to be studied. At the turn of the twentieth century, as today, the prevailing ideal of a "melting pot" could be either restrictive or progressive. In one sense, it entailed the imposition of Anglo-conformity on the immigrants, who were urged to cast off their "old world" cultures and embrace Americanism without delay. In a second, more liberal sense, this process of assimilation was capable of leveling the differences of ethnicity and religion between the various peoples of the United States; and, perhaps more important, it could transcend divisions of class between and within immigrant populations.

If the idea of a melting pot was always somewhat ambiguous, a more coherent version of the liberal ideal of assimilation was that of "cultural pluralism," a term coined by Horace M. Kallen in 1915, when the pressure for assimilation had hardened into a highly intolerant brand of "100 percent Americanism." The idea of cultural pluralism is usually expressed by the metaphor of a salad bowl or a symphony orchestra. In a salad, the lettuce is distinct from the tomatoes and the carrots, but together they make up a whole; in a symphony orchestra, all the instruments make different and even discordant sounds, but in unity they achieve harmony.

This central theme of assimilation is evident in the writings of the pioneer historian of U.S. immigration history, Marcus Hansen. He began his work on immigration by applying Frederick Jackson Turner's frontier thesis to the shaping of "the American character" as it absorbed diverse ethnic strains and immigrant groups. But, struck by the remarkable diversity of what he was describing, Hansen moved steadily to a position of cultural pluralism. Earlier Americans, he argued, had "made a bad blunder, when consciously or unconsciously they decreed that one literature, one attitude toward the arts, one set of standards should be the basis of culture." Why was the continent being reserved for one strain of Anglo-American culture, which had simply happened to settle in America first? Where this line of inquiry would have led Hansen is unclear, since he died young. But his fears and questions were certainly prescient, identifying dilemmas faced by the United States as the twentieth century draws to a close.

The Irish, among the most intensively studied of American immigrant groups, provide an example of the often contradictory choices facing a historian trying to understand the assimilation of a single ethnic group. Oscar Handlin, in his seminal social history of the Boston Irish, argues that the immigrants had a damaged, dysfunctional culture and their only hope of redemption was to cast off their old world customs and assimilate into the dominant mode of Anglo-conformity. There could be little room for cultural pluralism in this model. For Thomas Brown, on the other hand, the very commitment of Irish-Americans to the nationalist cause of freedom for Ireland insured their assimilation into the middle-class mainstream of American life. Pointing to the narrow social base of Brown's work, Eric Foner argues that Irish immigrant working men and women (in other words, the great majority of the immigrants) were assimilated into a radical, working-class alternative definition of America. This interpretation has been challenged by David Emmons, who finds little genuine or lasting radicalism among the Irish copper-workers of Butte, Montana; and by Kerby Miller, who concludes pessimistically, but on the basis of abundant and persuasive evidence, that a respectable Catholic middle class came to dominate the Irish community as a whole, overpowering more radical alternatives and insuring assimilation in an essentially bourgeois rather than radical manner.

Issues of race, gender, and culture enrich and complicate the debate still further. Hasia Diner and Janet Nolan have added a new dimension to the debate by explaining the distinctive way in which Irish women migrated, worked, and assimilated. More recently, David Roediger and Noel Ignatiev have argued that the precondition for Irish assimilation was to embrace the identity of "whiteness," thereby precluding potential interracial alliances among the most disadvantaged members of the labor force. The point here is not to blame the Irish so much as to expose the dilemmas facing immigrants and workers seeking to make a life for themselves in a society defined by race. Finally, Peter Way has added a radical, if still deeply pessimistic, twist to the Handlin thesis, emphasizing the damage inflicted on Irish culture by imperialism at home and capitalism abroad. Irish canal laborers in early-nineteenth-century America were so degraded and oppressed, Way concludes, that for them assimilation was not even an option.

The essential features of this debate are clearly relevant in understanding the assimilation of any immigrant group in America, not just the Irish. None of the models proposed will stand alone, and some are incompatible. What is needed is an account that pays due attention to the importance of religion; poverty and social mobility; pattern of migration and settlement; the interaction between newcomers and established members of the ethnic community; the hegemony of the middle class, both inside and outside the immigrant community; the potential for radical challenges to that hegemony; and the central questions of race and gender that recent historiography place at the heart of the study of immigration and ethnicity. In this respect, the work of Roediger and others suggests a particularly useful model for the study of ethnic and class identities, emphasizing how they were constructed in racial terms of "whiteness" and gendered terms of "masculinity." It is a model that can be applied as effectively to Mexicans in the twentieth century as to the Irish in the nineteenth.

It was difficult for the Irish to assimilate in nineteenth-century America, but clearly it was not impossible. By the time of the "new" immigration, they had been accorded, albeit grudgingly, the somewhat anomalous status of full Nordic Americans. But for other groups in American society in the late nineteenth and early twentieth centuries, most notably Latinos and Asians, "assimilation" took the form of subjugation and segregation, or was denied altogether through a policy of exclusion. By 1970, for example, one-third of all Puerto Ricans (almost 1.5 million) lived on the mainland, 817,712 of them in New York City, compared to only 463,242 in the island's capital, San Juan. Puerto Ricans have had U.S. citizenship since 1917, but this has not prevented them from being one of the most economically disadvantaged ethnic groups in the United States.

A similar, though quite distinctive pattern of discrimination is evident against Mexican Americans. The last century of Mexican American immigration has transformed the social, cultural, and political landscape of the Southwest. It has also been a period of systematic discrimination not only against Mexican immigrants but also against established Mexican Americans. Mexican labor quickly lost its indispensability when the American economy collapsed in the 1930s. Nearly half a million Mexicans were repatriated, some voluntarily and some coercively, as Camille Guerin-Gonzales and Abraham Hoffman have explained. In Texas and elsewhere, Mexican American citizens of the United States were subject to disfranchisement and a de facto Jim Crow system of segregation. In 1954, thousands of undocumented Mexican *braceros* were deported, under a government-organized program called "Operation Wetback."

Since 1960, Mexican immigration to the United States has grown at a faster pace than ever before. In 1990, the 20 million Latinos in the United States accounted for 9 percent of the country's population; 13.4 million of them were of Mexican origin, up from only 3.5 million in 1960. As the recent work of David Gutiérrez has persuasively demonstrated, the ongoing interaction between Chicanos and repeated waves of immigrants from Mexico calls into question the traditional dichotomy between citizen and alien at the heart of all models of assimilation. Mexican Americans have had a deeply ambivalent attitude toward newcomers from Mexico, on one hand embracing them in a transnational identity, on the other hand experiencing their presence as a cause of discrimination against themselves and an obstacle to assimilation. Within these tensions lie the makings of new, more fluid and dynamic categories of citizenship and ethnicity on both sides of the border.

That citizenship alone is no guarantee of civil and political rights is made clear in the history of Mexican Americans, Puerto Ricans, and African Americans, and even more starkly in the history of the Japanese Americans during World War II. In 1940 there were about 127,000 Americans of Japanese ancestry. Roughly one-third of them were unnaturalized first-generation immigrants, or issei; the other two-thirds were naturalized or native-born citizens of the United States, or nisei. Most Japanese Americans lived in California, others in Oregon, Washington, and Hawaii. John Modell has demonstrated the fragility of their position in society, a position that was to be severely undermined after war broke out between the United States and Japan in 1941. More than 100,000 Japanese Americans were forcibly "evacuated" to "relocation centers" in the interior during World War II, on the grounds that they represented a threat to national security. This harrowing tale, told most recently by Yuji Ichioka, Page Smith, and Michi Weglyn, offers a grim demonstration of the limits of tolerance and assimilation in twentieth-century America.

A WORLD IN MIGRATION: THE NEWEST IMMIGRANTS

As the United States approaches the twenty-first century, immigration has once again become a significant aspect of its history. Inspired by the Civil Rights and Voting Rights Acts, the Hart-Celler Act of 1965 abolished the old racial quota system; at the same time, however, it looked to the future by placing a limit on Latin American immigration for the first time. Under the new system, which went into effect in 1968, the annual ceiling was increased to 290,000: 170,000 from the Eastern Hemisphere (i.e., the rest of the world other than the Americas), with no more than 20,000 from any single county, and 120,000 from the Western Hemisphere. Provisions were made for special visas for refugees fleeing racial, political, and religious persecution (though not economic hardship), and more than 1 million refugees from Cuba and Indochina had arrived by 1980.

Before 1965, 90 percent of the annual immigrants to the United States were Europeans; by 1985, that figure had dropped to 10 percent. Between 1980 and 1990 alone, the number of Asians in the United States doubled, reaching more than 7 million. But the main source of immigration has been Latin America. Demographers estimate that by 2030, Americans of European origin will be in a minority, a situation that already pertains in New York City and in the California school system. This new wave of immigration is already receiving considerable scholarly attention. To take the ethnic mosaic of New York City as but one example, recent works attest to the continuing remarkable diversity of the metropolis: Hsiang-Shui Chen on immigrants from Taiwan, Philip Kasinitz on Caribbean immigrants and the politics of race, Illsoo Kim on the city's burgeoning Korean community, Peter Kwong on the new Chinatown, Michael Laguerre on the new Haitian community, and Nancy Foner's edited collection on immigrants, including Koreans, Chinese, Haitians, Soviet Jews, Dominicans, and Jamaicans and other Caribbean peoples. With a steady, two-way movement along the "Caribbean corridor," especially from Haiti, Jamaica, Puerto Rico, and the Dominican Republic, New York City—like the United States as a whole—is ethnically and racially more diverse than ever before.

Hand-in-hand with the proliferation of new immigrant groups since the 1960s has come a discovery of the concept of ethnicity by white Americans descended from previous immigrants. The more dogmatic versions of this "new white ethnicity" insist that the descendants of the Irish, the Italians and the Slavs have retained distinctive cultural and ethnic values without assimilating into the dominant Anglo-American culture. Inherent in this position, as Orlando Patterson has pointed out, is a reaction against the heightened race consciousness of African Americans and the social and political gains they have made since 1960.

While this form of ethnic chauvinism sees ethnicity as a fixed, almost primordial, essence, a final but as yet undeveloped strand of the historiography argues that ethnicity is a constructed and contested element of subjective identity. Compared to other fields in American history, the history of immigration and ethnicity has borrowed surprisingly little from discourse theory and the general "linguistic turn." Given the centrality of ethnicity as a category of subjective identity, however, the time is certainly ripe for such an approach. Werner Sollors has suggested a useful approach for analyzing ethnicity as a cultural construct, but the work has yet to go from a theoretical to an empirical level (in the writing of history at least, if not in literary studies).

At its most effective, the move to destabilize and historicize the category of ethnicity offers historians a powerful new tool, allowing them to expose the dynamics of power whereby immigrant communities are formed and reformed and ethnic identities defined and redefined. In particular, the ideological and discursive processes through which particular ethnic identities are constructed into categories of race and gender demand further attention. The best work in the future is likely to focus on the definition of ethnicity and assimilation by examining conflicts over resources, power, and culture between immigrants and the larger society they enter, between different ethnic and racial groups, and between different members of the same immigrant communities.

BIBLIOGRAPHY

Apart from older works discussed in the text, this list consists of a representative selection of works published since 1980.

General Studies and Surveys

Archdeacon, Thomas. *Becoming American: An Ethnic History.* New York: Free Press, 1983.
Bayor, Ronald H., and Timothy J. Meagher, eds. *The New York Irish.* Baltimore, Md.: Johns Hopkins University Press, 1996.
Bennett, David H. *The Party of Fear: From Nativist Movements to the New Right in American History.* Chapel Hill: University of North Carolina Press, 1988.

Bodnar, John E. *The Transplanted: A History of Immigrants in Urban America.* Bloomington: University of Indiana Press, 1985.
Buckowczyk, John J. *And My Children Did Not Know Me: A History of the Polish-Americans.* Bloomington: Indiana University Press, 1987.
Chan, Sucheng. *Asian-Americans: An Interpretive History.* Boston: Twayne, 1991.
Daniels, Roger. *Asian America: Chinese and Japanese in the United States since 1850.* Seattle: University of Washington Press, 1988.
Del Castillo, Adelaida R., ed. *Between Borders: Essays on Mexicana/Chicana History.* Encino, Calif.: Floricanto Press, 1990.
Golab, Caroline. *Immigrant Destinations.* Philadelphia: Temple University Press, 1977.
Hansen, Marcus. *The Atlantic Migration, 1607–1860.* Cambridge, Mass.: Harvard University Press, 1940.
———. *The Immigrant in American History.* New York: Harper Torchbooks, 1940.
Ichioka, Yuji. *The Issei: The World of the First-Generation Japanese Immigrants, 1885–1924.* New York: Free Press, 1988.
Miller, Kerby A. *Emigrants and Exiles: Ireland and the Irish Exodus to North America.* New York: Oxford University Press, 1985.
Montejano, David. *Anglos and Mexicans in the Making of Texas, 1836–1986.* Austin: University of Texas Press, 1987.
Patterson, Orlando. *Ethnic Chauvinism: The Reactionary Impulse.* New York: Stein & Day, 1977.
Sollors, Werner, *Beyond Ethnicity: Consent and Descent in American Culture.* New York: Oxford University Press, 1986.
———, ed. *The Invention of Ethnicity.* New York: Oxford University Press, 1989.
Takaki, Ronald T. *Strangers from a Different Shore: A History of Asian Americans.* Boston: Little, Brown, 1989.
Thernstrom, Stephan, Ann Orlov, and Oscar Handlin, eds. *Harvard Encyclopedia of American Ethnic Groups.* Cambridge, Mass.: Harvard University Press, 1980.
Yans-McLaughlin, Virginia, ed. *Immigration Reconsidered: History, Sociology, and Politics.* New York: Oxford University Press, 1990.

Immigration and Ethnicity in Early America

Bailyn, Bernard. *The Peopling of British North America: An Introduction.* New York: Knopf, 1985.
———. *Voyagers to the West: A Passage in the Peopling of America on the Eve of the Revolution.* New York: Knopf, 1986.
Bailyn, Bernard, and Philip D. Morgan, eds. *Strangers within the Realm: Cultural Margins of the First British Empire.* Chapel Hill: University of North Carolina Press, 1991.
Balmer, Randall H. *A Perfect Babel of Confusions: Dutch Religion and English Culture in the Middle Colonies.* New York: Oxford University Press, 1989.
Bannon, John F. *The Spanish Borderlands Frontier, 1513–1821.* Albuquerque: University of New Mexico Press, 1974.
Butler, Jon. *The Huguenots in America: A Refugee People in a New World Society.* Cambridge, Mass.: Harvard University Press, 1983.

Ethnicity and Immigration

Ekirch, A. Roger. *Bound for America: The Transportation of British Convicts to the Colonies, 1718–1775.* New York: Oxford University Press, 1987.

Fischer, David Hackett. *Albion's Seed: Four British Folkways in America.* New York: Oxford University Press, 1989.

Galenson, David W. *White Servitude in Colonial America: An Economic Analysis.* New York: Cambridge University Press, 1981.

Goodfriend, Joyce D. *Before the Melting Pot: Society and Culture in Colonial New York City, 1664–1730.* Princeton, N.J.: Princeton University Press, 1992.

Gutiérrez, Ramón A. *When Jesus Came, the Corn Mothers Went Away: Marriage, Sexuality, and Power in New Mexico, 1500–1846.* Stanford, Calif.: Stanford University Press, 1991.

Kettner, James H. *The Development of American Citizenship, 1608–1870.* Chapel Hill: University of North Carolina Press, 1978.

Swierenga, Robert. *The Dutch in America: Immigration, Settlement, and Cultural Change.* New Brunswick, N.J.: Rutgers University Press, 1985.

Nineteenth Century to 1890

Brown, Thomas N. *Irish-American Nationalism, 1870–1890.* Philadelphia: Lippincott, 1966.

Craver, Rebecca. *The Impact of Intimacy: Mexican-Anglo Intermarriage in New Mexico, 1821–1846.* El Paso: Texas Western Press, University of Texas, 1982.

De Léon, Arnoldo. *They Called Them Greasers: Anglo-American Attitudes toward Mexicans in Texas, 1821–1900.* Austin: University of Texas Press, 1983.

Diner, Hasia. *Erin's Daughters in America: Irish Immigrant Women in the Nineteenth Century.* Baltimore, Md.: Johns Hopkins University Press, 1983.

Dolan, Jay P. *The Immigrant Church: New York's German and Irish Catholics, 1815–1865.* Baltimore, Md.: Johns Hopkins University Press, 1987.

Foner, Eric. "Class, Ethnicity, and Radicalism in the Gilded Age: The Land League and Irish America." *Marxist Perspectives* 1 (summer 1978): 6–55.

Gutman, Herbert. *Work, Culture, and Society in Industrializing America: Essays in American Working-Class History.* New York: Vintage Books, 1977.

Handlin, Oscar. *Boston's Immigrants, 1790–1880: A Study in Acculturation.* Rev. ed. Cambridge, Mass.: Belknap Press of Harvard University Press, 1959. Reprint, New York: Atheneum, 1976.

Hinojosa, Gilberto. *A Borderlands Town in Transition: Laredo, 1755–1870.* College Station: Texas A&M University Press, 1983.

Ignatiev, Noel. *How the Irish Became White.* New York: Routledge, 1995.

Kamphoefner, Walter D. *The Westfalians: From Germany to Missouri.* Princeton, N.J.: Princeton University Press, 1987.

Knobel, Dale T. *Paddy and the Republic: Ethnicity and Nationality in Antebellum America.* Middletown, Conn.: Wesleyan University Press, 1986.

Levine, Bruce. *The Spirit of 1848: German Immigrants, Labor Conflict, and the Coming of the Civil War.* Urbana: University of Illinois Press, 1992.

Nadel, Stanley. *Little Germany: Ethnicity, Religion, and Class in New York City, 1845–1880.* Urbana: University of Illinois Press, 1990.

Roediger, David. *The Wages of Whiteness: Race and the Making of the American Working Class.* New York: Verso, 1991.
Saxton, Alexander P. *The Indispensable Enemy: Labor and the Anti-Chinese Movement in California.* Berkeley: University of California Press, 1971.
Takaki, Ronald. *Iron Cages: Race and Culture in Nineteenth-Century America.* New York: Oxford University Press, 1990.
Trommler, Frank, and Joseph McVeigh, eds. *America and the Germans: An Assessment of a Three-Hundred-Year History.* 2 vols. Philadelphia: University of Pennsylvania Press, 1985.
Turbin, Carole. *Working Women of the Collar City: Gender, Class, and Community in Troy, New York, 1864–86.* Urbana: University of Illinois Press, 1992.
Way, Peter. *Common Labour: Workers and the Digging of North American Canals, 1780–1860.* New York: Cambridge University Press, 1993.

Late Nineteenth and Twentieth Century

Acuña, Rodolfo. *A Community Under Siege: A Chronicle of Chicanos East of the Los Angeles River.* Los Angeles: Chicano Studies Research Center, University of California, 1984.
Bodnar, John E. *Immigration and Industrialization: Ethnicity in an American Mill Town, 1870–1940.* Pittsburgh, Pa.: University of Pittsburgh Press, 1977.
———. *Workers' World: Kinship, Community, and Protest in Industrial Society, 1900–1940.* Baltimore, Md.: Johns Hopkins University Press, 1982.
Bodnar, John E., Roger Simon, and Michael Weber. *Lives of Their Own: Blacks, Italians, and Poles in Pittsburgh, 1900–1960.* Urbana: University of Illinois Press, 1982.
Bonacich, Edna, and Ivan Light. *Immigrant Entrepreneurs: Koreans in Los Angeles, 1965–82.* Berkeley: University of California Press, 1988.
Brumberg, Stephan F. *Going to America, Going to School: The Jewish Immigrant Public School Encounter in Turn-of-the-Century New York City.* New York: Praeger, 1986.
Camarillo, Albert. *Chicanos in a Changing Society: From Mexican Pueblos to American Barrios in Santa Barbara and Southern California, 1848–1930.* Cambridge, Mass.: Harvard University Press, 1979.
Caroli, Betty Boyd. *Italian Repatriation from the United States, 1900–1914.* New York: Center for Migration Studies, 1973.
Chan, Sucheng, ed. *Entry Denied: Exclusion and the Chinese Community in America, 1882–1943.* Philadelphia: Temple University Press, 1991.
Chavez, John. *The Lost Land: The Chicano Image of the Southwest.* Albuquerque: University of New Mexico Press, 1984.
Chen, Hsiang-Shui. *Chinatown No More: Taiwan Immigrants in Contemporary New York.* Ithaca, N.Y.: Cornell University Press, 1992.
Deutsch, Sarah. *No Separate Refuge: Culture, Class, and Gender on an Anglo-Hispanic Frontier in the American Southwest, 1880–1940.* New York: Oxford University Press, 1987.
Emmons, David M. *The Butte Irish: Class and Ethnicity in an American Mining Town, 1875–1925.* Urbana: University of Illinois Press, 1989.

Ewen, Elizabeth. *Immigrant Women in the Land of Dollars: Life and Culture on the Lower East Side, 1890–1925.* New York: Monthly Review Press, 1985.

Fawcett, James, and Benjamin Carino, eds. *Pacific Bridges: The New Immigration from Asia and the Pacific Islands.* New York: Center for Migration Studies, 1987.

Foner, Nancy, ed. *New Immigrants in New York.* New York: Columbia University Press, 1987.

Gabaccia, Donna R. *From Sicily to Elizabeth Street: Housing and Social Change among Italian Immigrants, 1880–1930.* Albany: State University of New York Press, 1983.

———. *Militants and Migrants: Rural Sicilians Become American Workers.* New Brunswick, N.J.: Rutgers University Press, 1988.

Garcia, Juan Ramón. *Operation Wetback: The Mass Deportation of Mexican Undocumented Workers in 1954.* Westport, Conn.: Greenwood Press, 1980.

Garcia, Mario T. *Desert Immigrants: The Mexicans of El Paso, 1880–1920.* New Haven, Conn.: Yale University Press, 1981.

———. *Mexican Americans: Leadership, Ideology and Identity, 1930–1960.* New Haven, Conn.: Yale University Press, 1989.

Gerstle, Gary. *Working-Class Americanism: The Politics of Labor in a Textile City, 1914–1960.* New York: Cambridge University Press, 1989.

Glenn, Susan. *Daughters of the Shtetl: Life and Labor in the Immigrant Generation.* Ithaca, N.Y.: Cornell University Press, 1990.

Goldberg, David W. *A Tale of Three Cities: Labor Organization and Protest in Patterson, Passaic, and Lawrence, 1916–1921.* New Brunswick, N.J.: Rutgers University Press, 1989.

Greene, Victor. *The Slavic Community on Strike: Immigrant Labor in Pennsylvania Anthracite.* Notre Dame, Ind.: University of Notre Dame Press, 1968.

Griswold del Castillo, Richard. *La Familia: Chicano Families in the Urban Southwest, 1848 to the Present.* Notre Dame, Ind.: University of Notre Dame Press, 1984.

———. *The Los Angeles Barrio: A Social History.* Berkeley: University of California Press, 1979.

Guerin-Gonzales, Camille. *Mexican Workers, American Dreams: Immigration, Repatriation, and California Farm Labor, 1900–1939.* New Brunswick, N.J.: Rutgers University Press, 1994.

Gutiérrez, David G. *Walls and Mirrors: Mexican Americans, Mexican Immigrants, and the Politics of Ethnicity.* Berkeley: University of California Press, 1995.

Hareven, Tamara. *Family Time and Industrial Time: The Relationship between Family and Work in a New England Industrial Community.* New York: Cambridge University Press, 1982.

Higham, John. *Strangers in the Land: Patterns of American Nativism, 1860–1925.* 1963. New York: Atheneum Books, 1977.

Hoerder, Dirk, ed. *Struggle a Hard Battle: Essays on Working-Class Immigrants.* DeKalb: Northern Illinois University Press, 1986.

———, ed. *European Migrants: Global and Local Perspectives.* Boston: Northeastern University Press, 1996.

———, ed. *Labor Migration in the Atlantic Economies: The European and North Amer-*

ican Working Classes during the Period of Industrialization. Westport, Conn.: Greenwood Press, 1985.
Hoffman, Abraham. *Unwanted Mexican Americans in the Great Depression: Repatriation Pressures, 1929–1939.* Tucson: University of Arizona Press, 1974.
Hosakawa, Bill. *Nisei: The Quiet Americans.* New York: Morrow, 1969.
Howe, Irving, with Kenneth Libo. *World of Our Fathers: The Journey of East European Jews to America and the Life They Found and Made.* New York: Harcourt Brace Jovanovich, 1976.
Ichioka, Yuji, ed. *Views from Within: The Japanese American Evacuation and Relocation.* Los Angeles: Asian American Studies Center, University of California, 1989.
Jensen, Joan M. *Passage from India: Asian Indian Immigrants in North America.* New Haven, Conn.: Yale University Press, 1988.
Kasinitz, Philip. *Caribbean New York: Black Immigrants and the Politics of Race.* Ithaca, N.Y.: Cornell University Press, 1992.
Keil, Hartmut, and John B. Jentz, eds. *German Workers in Industrial Chicago, 1850–1910: A Comparative Perspective.* DeKalb: Northern Illinois University Press, 1983.
Kim, Illsoo. *New Urban Immigrants: The Korean Community in New York City.* Princeton, N.J.: Princeton University Press, 1981.
Kitano, H. L., and Roger Daniels. *Asian-Americans: Emerging Minorities.* 2d ed. Englewood Cliffs, N.J.: Prentice-Hall, 1988.
Krause, Paul. *The Battle for Homestead, 1880–1892: Politics, Culture and Steel.* Pittsburgh, Pa.: University of Pittsburgh Press, 1992.
Kwong, Peter. *The New Chinatown.* New York: Hill & Wang, 1987.
Laguerre, Michael. *American Odyssey: Haitians in New York City.* Ithaca, N.Y.: Cornell University Press, 1984.
Modell, John. *The Economics and Politics of Racial Accommodation: The Japanese of Los Angeles, 1900–1942.* Urbana: University of Illinois Press, 1977.
Montgomery, David. *The Fall of the House of Labor: The Workplace, the State, and American Labor Activism, 1865–1925.* New York: Cambridge University Press, 1987.
Moore, Deborah Dash. *At Home in America: Second Generation New York Jews.* New York: Columbia University Press, 1981.
Mora, Magdalena, and Adelaida R. Del Castillo, eds. *Mexican Women in the United States: Struggles Past and Present.* Los Angeles: Chicano Studies Research Center, University of California, 1980.
Moraskawa, Ewa. *For Bread with Butter: Life-Worlds of East Central Europeans in Johnstown, Pennsylvania, 1890–1940.* New York: Cambridge University Press, 1986.
Muller, Thomas, and Thomas J. Espenshade. *The Fourth Wave: California's Newest Immigrants.* Washington, D.C.: The Urban Institute, 1985.
Novak, Michael. *The Rise of the Unmeltable Ethnics: Politics and Culture in the Seventies.* New York: Macmillan, 1972.
Nolan, Janet. *Ourselves Alone: Women's Immigration from Ireland, 1885–1920.* Lexington: University Press of Kentucky, 1989.

Orsi, Robert. *The Madonna of 115th Street: Faith and Community in Italian Harlem, 1880–1950.* New Haven, Conn.: Yale University Press, 1985.

Ostergren, Robert. *A Community Transplanted: The Transatlantic Experience of a Swedish Immigrant Settlement in the Upper Middle West, 1835–1915.* Madison: University of Wisconsin Press, 1988.

Patterson, Orlando. *Ethnic Chauvinism: The Reactionary Impulse.* New York: Stein & Day, 1977.

Rischin, Moses. *The Promised City: New York's Jews, 1870–1914.* Cambridge, Mass.: Harvard University Press, 1962.

Rodriguez, Richard. *Hunger of Memory: The Education of Richard Rodriguez.* Boston: D. R. Godine, 1981.

Romo, Ricardo. *East Los Angeles: History of a Barrio.* Austin: University of Texas Press, 1983.

Ruiz, Vicki. *Cannery Women, Cannery Lives: Mexican Women, Unionization, and the California Food Processing Industry.* Albuquerque: University of New Mexico Press, 1987.

Ruiz, Vicki, and Susan Tiano, eds. *Women on the U.S.-Mexico Border: Responses to Change.* Boston: Allen & Unwin, 1987.

Saran, Parmatma. *The Asian Indian Experience in the United States.* Cambridge, Mass.: Schenkman, 1985.

Smith, Page. *Democracy on Trial: The Japanese-American Evacuation and Relocation in World War II.* New York: Simon & Schuster, 1995.

Tomasi, Silvano. *Piety and Power: The Role of Italian Parishes in the New York Metropolitan Area, 1880–1930.* New York: Center for Migration Studies, 1975.

Vargas, Zaragosa. *Proletarians of the North: A History of Mexican Industrial Workers in Detroit and the Midwest, 1917–1933.* Berkeley: University of California Press, 1993.

Weglyn, Michi. *Years of Infamy: The Untold Story of America's Concentration Camps.* New York: Morrow, 1976.

Weinberg, Sydney. *The World of Our Mothers: Lives of Jewish Immigrant Women.* Chapel Hill: University of North Carolina Press, 1988.

Weisser, Michael R. *A Brotherhood of Memory: Jewish Landsmanshaftn in the New York World.* New York: Basic Books, 1985.

Yans-McLaughlin, Virginia. *Family and Community: Italian Immigrants in Buffalo, 1880–1930.* Ithaca, N.Y.: Cornell University Press, 1977.

Zamora, Emilio. *The World of the Mexican Workers in Texas.* College Station: Texas A&M University Press, 1993.